Lullabies & Good Night

A Collection of Classic Lullaby Poetry

Lyrical adaptations of poems by
Stephen Elkins

Illustrated with the art of
Mary Cassatt

IDEALS CHILDREN'S BOOKS
Nashville, Tennessee

Copyright © 1989 by Ideals Publishing Corporation
All rights reserved.
Published by Ideals Publishing Corporation
Nashville, Tennessee
Printed and bound in the United States of America.
ISBN 0-8249-7351-8 BK

A Cradle Song

What does little birdie say
In her nest at peep of day?
Let me fly, says little birdie,
Mother, let me fly away.

Birdie, rest a little longer,
Till the little wings are stronger.
So she rests a little longer;
Then she flies away.

What does little baby say
In her bed at peep of day?
Baby says, like little birdie,
Let me rise and fly away!

Baby, sleep a little longer,
Till the little limbs are stronger.
If she sleeps a little longer,
Baby too shall fly away.

Alfred, Lord Tennyson

Emily

Emily, Emily, Emily, Emily, I love you.
Emily, Emily, Emily, Emily, I love you.

Where are you, my sweet Emily? The night is falling.
Where are you, my sweet Emily? Your mother's calling.
Oh, come to bed and lay your head upon my shoulder.
What joy I feel! I should be still, but again I told her,

Emily, Emily, Emily, Emily, I love you.
Emily, Emily, Emily, Emily, I love you.

The angels, my sweet Emily, are here beside you;
And heaven, my sweet Emily, will always guide you.
I love you so! You'll never know the joy you're bringing.
This love inside, no one could hide, so again I'm singing,

Emily, Emily, Emily, Emily, I love you.
Emily, Emily, Emily, Emily, I love you.

Stephen Elkins

Mary Cassatt; **Baby Reaching for an Apple** 1893; Virginia Museum of Fine Arts, Richmond, Virginia

Mary Cassatt; **Maternal Kiss**, 1897; 52-82-11 Philadelphia Museum of Art; Bequest of Anne Hinchman

Good Night

Little baby, lay your head
Upon your pretty cradle bed
And shut your eye-peeps now that day
And all the light have gone away.

Yes, my sweet darling, well I know
How the bitter wind doth blow;
And the winter's snow and rain
Patter on the windowpane.

Little baby, lay your head
Upon your pretty cradle bed
And shut your eye-peeps now that day
And all the light have gone away.

For the window shuts so fast
Till the stormy night is past,
And the curtains warm are spread
Round about your cradle bed.

Little baby, lay your head
Upon your pretty cradle bed
And shut your eye-peeps now that day
And all the light have gone away.

Jane Taylor

Cradle Hymn

Hush, my dear, lie still and slumber;
Holy angels guard thy bed,
Heavenly blessings without number
Gently falling on thy head.

How much better thou'rt attended
Than the Son of God could be
When from heaven he descended
And became a child like thee.

May you live to know and fear him,
Trust and love him all thy days,
Then go dwell forever near him,
See his face and sing his praise.

How much better thou'rt attended
Than the Son of God could be
When from heaven he descended
And became a child like thee.

I could give thee thousand kisses,
Hoping what I most desire;
Not a mother's fondest wishes
Can to greater joys aspire.

How much better thou'rt attended
Than the Son of God could be
When from heaven he descended
And became a child like thee.

Isaac Watts

Mary Cassatt, American 1844-1926; **Women Admiring a Child,** 1897; pastel, 26 x 32 in.; Accession No. 08.8;© The Detroit Institute of Arts; Gift of Edward Chandler Walker

My Little White Lamb

Green are the pastures of Sleepy Land;
Fresh are the fields and fair;
Wide are the ways to its wonder-fold,
And my little white lamb is there.

O tall Dream Shepherd, I pray you hear,
Fair though your pastures be,
Let down the bars and bring once more
My little white lamb to me.

Blue are the skies over Sleepy Land;
Clear are the brooks and bright;
With a Shepherd Dream to the slumber gate
Went my little white lamb last night.

O tall Dream Shepherd, I pray you hear,
Fair though your pastures be,
And let down the bars and bring once more
My little white lamb to me.

Grace Duffield Goodwin

Mary Cassatt; **Poppies in a Field**. c. 1874-1880; 1978-1-6 Philadelphia Museum of Art; Bequest of Charlotte Dorrance Wright

Children Playing on the Beach, 1884, Mary Cassatt; National Gallery of Art, Washington, D.C.; Ailsa Mellon Bruce Collection

Mother's Song

My heart is like a fountain true
That flows and flows with love to you.
As chirps the lark unto the tree,
So chirps my pretty babe to me.

And it's oh, sweet, sweet;
And it's oh, sweet, sweet;
And it's oh, sweet, sweet;
My baby's lullaby.

There's not a star that shines on high
Is brighter than my baby's eye.
There's not a boat upon the sea
Can dance as baby does to me.

And it's oh, sweet, sweet;
And it's oh, sweet, sweet;
And it's oh, sweet, sweet;
My baby's lullaby.

English Lullaby

Mary Cassatt; **Maternal Caress**, 1896; 70-75-2 Philadelphia Museum of Art; Gift of Aaron Carpenter

The Poppy Land Express

The first train leaves at six P.M.
For the land where the poppies do grow;
And mother dear is the brave engineer,
And the passenger laughs and crows.

So I ask of Him who the children took
On His knee in His kindness so great:
"Take charge, I pray, of the trains every day
That are leaving at six and eight."

The palace car is my mother's arms,
And the whistle is a low, sweet strain.
The passenger winks and then nods and then blinks
And then goes to sleep in the train.

So I ask of Him who the children took
On His knee in His kindness so great:
"Take charge, I pray, of the trains every day
That are leaving at six and eight."

Edgar Wade Abbott

Mary Cassatt; **The Bath**, 1891-92; oil on canvas, 39½ in. x 26 in.; Robert Waller Fund, 1910.2; © 1988 The Art Institute of Chicago. All Rights Reserved.

The Road to Slumber Land

What is the road to Slumber Land?
Tell me, when does the baby go?
The road is so straight through Mother's arms,
And the sun is sinking low.

This is the way, through Mother's arms,
All little babies go.
This is the road to Slumber Land
When the sun is sinking low.

Soft little gown so clean and white
And a face washed so sweet and fair —
A mother with love is brushing out
All the tangles in baby's hair.

This is the way, through Mother's arms,
All little babies go.
This is the road to Slumber Land
When the sun is sinking low.

Mary D. Brine

Tucking the Baby In

The dark, heavy eyelids slowly close
On eyes serene and deep;
Upon my breast my own sweet child
Has gently dropped to sleep.

And oh, how fair, how innocent,
Like some sweet angel strayed!
Oh, how fair, how innocent,
That slumbers unafraid.

I kiss his soft and dimpled cheek;
I kiss his rounded chin,
Then lay him on his little bed
And tuck my baby in.

And oh, how fair, how innocent,
Like some sweet angel strayed!
Oh, how fair, how innocent,
That slumbers unafraid.

Curtis May

Mary Cassatt; **Breakfast in Bed;** Courtesy Henry E. Huntington Library and Art Gallery, San Marino, California, Virginia Steele Scott Collection

Sweet and Low

Sweet and low, sweet and low,
Wind of the western sea does blow.
Sweet and low, sweet and low,
Wind of the western sea does blow.

Over the rolling waters go,
Come from the dropping moon, and blow,
Blow him again to me while my little one,
While my pretty one sleeps tonight.

Sweet and low, sweet and low,
Wind of the western sea does blow.
Sweet and low, sweet and low,
Wind of the western sea does blow.

Sleep and rest, sleep and rest,
Rest on your loving mother's breast.
Sleep and rest, sleep and rest,
Rest on your loving mother's breast.

Father will come to his babe in the nest
Like silver sails out of the west;
Under the silver moon, sleep, my little one,
Sleep, my little one, sleep tonight.

Sleep and rest, sleep and rest,
Rest on your loving mother's breast.
Sleep and rest, sleep and rest,
Rest on your loving mother's breast.

Alfred, Lord Tennyson

Mary Cassatt, **Family Group Reading**, 1901; 42-102-1 Philadelphia Museum of Art; Given by Mr. and Mrs. J. Watson Webb.

Sleep, Little Tulip, Sleep

The mill goes toiling slowly around
With steady and solemn creak,
And my little one hears a song in the sound,
The voice of the old mill speak.

Round and round those big white wings
Grimly and ghostlike creep;
My little one hears the old mill sing,
"Sleep, little tulip, sleep!"

The sails are reefed, the nets they are drawn,
And over his pot of tea,
The fisher, against the morrow's dawn,
Happily sings for me.

Round and round those big white wings
Grimly and ghostlike creep;
My little one hears the old mill sing,
"Sleep, little tulip, sleep!"

Eugene Field